T0167840

BRITAIN'S 🏰 HERITAGE

Seaside Hotels

Karen Averby

AMBERLEY

Acknowledgements

Warm thanks and appreciation are extended to those who have contributed their fantastic images for this publication. As ever, I am grateful to the various archives and museums I have visited or been in touch with during the course of research, the following in particular: Conwy Archives (especially Susan Ellis), Dorset History Centre, Ilfracombe Museum (special thanks to Sara Hodson), The National Archives, Ceredigion Museum, Suffolk Record Office, and the Victoria and Albert Museum. Many enjoyable and interesting experiences were had while researching for this book, notably during visits to various grand hotels along the way. Thanks are due to many of the hotel staff encountered, especially reception staff, and in particular those at the Palace Hotel, Paignton; the Grand Hotel, Torquay (thank you, Dawn); Headland Hotel, Torquay; Premier Inn Bournemouth Central; and Royal Hotel, Weymouth, as well as for hospitality received at Brighton's Metropole. Genevieve Bovee deserves an extra special mention for being super-sterling, as does my editor Nick Wright, and extra thanks too to KvS, WTR and TLS for the cheers. The fabulous Patricia Pradey, Michelle Doig and Jenny Guest are appreciated as ever, and finally, the big special thanks are reserved for Jay Garret, interminably-A.

The author gratefully acknowledges the permission granted to reproduce the copyright material in this book. Every effort has been made to trace copyright holders and to obtain their permission for the use of copyright material.

Images 6, 15, 17, 29, 41, 44, 58, 69, 73, 74, 75, 76 are copyrighted but licensed for further reuse under Creative Commons Attribution-ShareAlike 2.0 Generic (CC BY-SA 2.0)

Images 5 and 34 are reproduced under Creative Commons Public Domain Mark 1.0

Image 21 is reproduced under Creative Commons CC BY-SA 3.0

Images 30 and 31 are reproduced under Creative Commons Attribution 4.0 International (CC BY 4.0)

Image 77 is reproduced under Attribution 2.0 Generic (CC BY 2.0)

Unless listed above, uncredited images are usually attributable to the author or derive from the author's collection.

Cover image: Queens Hotel, Eastbourne. (ian woolcock/Shutterstock.com)

First published 2018

Amberley Publishing
The Hill, Stroud
Gloucestershire, GL5 4EP

www.amberley-books.com

Copyright © Karen Averby, 2018

The right of Karen Averby to be identified as the Author of this work has been asserted in accordance with the Copyrights, Designs and Patents Act 1988.

ISBN 978 1 4456 7546 6 (paperback)
ISBN 978 1 4456 7547 3 (ebook)

All rights reserved. No part of this book may be reprinted or reproduced or utilised in any form or by any electronic, mechanical or other means, now known or hereafter invented, including photocopying and recording, or in any information storage or retrieval system, without the permission in writing from the Publishers.

British Library Cataloguing in Publication Data.
A catalogue record for this book is available from the British Library.

Printed in the UK.

Contents

1

Introduction

The grand seaside hotel is characteristically situated in a prominent location, usually on the seafront or atop imposing cliffs commanding magnificent views across the water. Sometimes presenting a faded grandeur, sometimes resplendently restored, grand hotels are visually dominant within the seaside landscape. They form part of a long tradition of accommodation provided for coastal visitors over the last 300 years, from humble beginnings in fishermen's cottages to today's multi-million pound seaside hospitality and leisure industry. Along the way the grand hotel has provided luxury accommodation in opulent surroundings for those who could afford it, built in the architectural styles of the day; the hybrid and mannered hotels of the Regency paved the way for Victorian monumentality, Edwardian flamboyance, inter-war Art Deco magnificence and finally the blander blockishness of more recent periods as corporate image began to dominate.

The diversity of architectural styles and forms of the seaside hotel was influenced by changes in architectural fashion, society, patterns of holidaying, and attitudes to nature. They are integral to the character of individual resorts, their locations and form dictated by topography and landscape, their construction always financially motivated, their survival dependent upon attracting and retaining guests.

Until the eighteenth century the coast was very much the domain of fisherman and other sea-faring folk, and visiting for leisure and pleasure was unheard of. A transformation in

the way the coast was used and perceived began in the seventeenth century when a desire for improved health and a belief in the therapeutic and curative nature of the seaside led to the development of the first coastal resorts in the eighteenth century. As inland spa resorts had become fashionable among the upper echelons of society, so too did sea resorts, where the medicinal cure-all properties of sea water were promoted by prominent physicians. The practice of sea bathing in particular gained popularity as part of the growing pursuit of health, leisure and pleasure amongst wealthy, fashionable society and by the 1730s sea bathing seasons were emerging at Scarborough, Margate and Brighton.

The grandiose Grand Hotel, Scarborough. Completed in 1867, it was the largest brick structure in Europe at that time. It dominates its environs with its ornamental domes forming a dramatic skyline. (travellight/Shutterstock.com)

Above: The Royal Hotel, Weymouth, opened in 1899 on the site of an earlier 1770s hotel of the same name. Constructed in red brick with Portland stone dressings, it is typical of many buildings of the period. (Jay Garrett)

Right: Queens Hotel, Eastbourne, opened in 1880. Designed by Henry Currey, who had been articled to Decimus Burton, it took just eleven months to construct and is an iconic and prominent building on the seafront. (Lara Band)

The Midland Hotel, Morecambe. Built in 1933, it had become derelict by the turn of the twenty-first century, but was saved from demolition and restored to its former glory by developers Urban Splash, reopening in 2008. (Chris Coates, Morecambe)

Engraving of Scarborough, by John Setterington, 1735. Scarborough had been visited as a spa town since the seventeenth century and developed as a seaside resort from the 1720s. This shows the earliest known depiction of a bathing machine.

Clarence House, North Street, Brighton. Built in 1785 as the New Inn, providing 'Lodgings, & Apartments for Gentlemen & Families,' it was renamed the Clarence Hotel in 1830 and remained a hotel until 1972. (Rob Bourn)

The relatively remote locations of these small, early resorts and the often hazardous and long coach journeys required to reach them meant that accommodation was essential. Existing private dwellings were initially used, often small cottages renovated for the purpose, and inns began to spring up, as at Brighton, Scarborough, Weymouth and Ramsgate. Early inns were often small, dirty, uncomfortable and unsuited to long stays, so it was often preferable to stay for as short a time as possible while suitable private lodgings were found. Changing concepts concerning accommodation away from home began to emerge; although coaching inns and post houses had hitherto provided short-term rudimentary shelter, warmth and refreshment during a journey, purpose-built establishments at a desirable end location offering more comfort were a different and new notion.

Trade and prosperity arising from the growth of fashionable watering places encouraged new building and by the later eighteenth century, as coastal resorts grew from small settlements, lines of fine grand houses were purpose-built as seasonal accommodation. These were either for the use of those who built them and their friends and acquaintances, or else were intended to be leased to the fashionable set, offering suites of rooms or the entire residence for the very wealthy.

Did you know?

In 1780 the Duke of Gloucester commissioned a house to be built in Weymouth. Later known as Gloucester Lodge, his brother George III stayed there in 1789 when he visited the resort to recuperate from a severe bout of incapacity.

In time many inns raised standards to rival the private homes being leased. As the word 'hotel' came to be used for these better quality inns, establishments advertising themselves as such began to appear at resorts such as Blackpool, Margate and Brighton. By 1785 Lawrence Bailey of Blackpool was regularly advertising his Bailey's Hotel in the *Manchester Mercury*, and by 1791 the London Hotel, Ramsgate, was proudly proclaiming itself as being 'furnished in genteel stile all entire new furniture and beds the best quality.' The first resort guidebooks were published from the mid-eighteenth century, promoting resorts for health and leisure with details of fashionable entertainment and accommodation within, which allowed reservations to be made in advance.

MITCHENER

New Inn and Hotel,

MARGATE.

On the PARADE, by the *Water Side.*

HAVING rebuilt, on a much improved Plan, and confiderably enlarged his Houfe, folicits the Support and Favour of the Nobility, Gentry, and Public in general, to whofe Commands the greateft Attention will be paid; and he begs Leave to inform them, that Families or fingle Gentlemen may be accommodated with Lodging and Board, at his NEW HOTEL, on any Plan agreeable to themfelves.—His Stock of Wines are exceedingly choice, and of the highest Flavour; his other Liquors the beft that can be procured; his Larder conftantly fupplied with every Thing in Seafon, the beft of the Kind; his new Buildings command a moft extenfive and delightful Profpect, and no Expence has been fpared to fit up the fame in a Manner fuitable for the Reception of his Friends.—Their Situation renders them particularly convenient for Sea bathing; his Machines are in the neateft Stile, and provided with careful Attendants.—He has alfo Marble Salt-water Baths within his own Buildings.

His Diligences and Coaches run to and from LONDON every Day; alfo Poft-coaches and Poft-chaifes to any Part of ENGLAND.

☞ The above INN is moft conveniently fituated for Paffengers to embark on Board the Veffels that Sail to OSTEND, or any foreign Parts.

Left: Advertisement of 1783 for the rebuilt and enlarged Mitchener Hotel, Margate, aimed at families or single gentlemen. Its attractions included wines, liquors, salt water baths and sea bathing machines. *(Kentish Gazette,* 11 June 1783)

Below: Royal Pier Hotel, Ryde, c. 1905. Built shortly after the new pier of 1814 to accommodate the extra influx of passengers, it formed part of Pier Street with other buildings. All were demolished following a fatal bus crash in 1930.

The era of the modern seaside hotel, rather than an inn, emerged as individuals recognised a need for specialist establishments providing more luxurious accommodation for those who could afford it. These early incarnations were essentially houses providing a suite of rooms or apartments for wealthy patrons and their servants, often with private sitting rooms and coffee rooms. Unlike coaching inns there was no early rising requirement, nor were these establishments available for the general public; rooms and facilities were for the exclusive use of guests. Resorts did not have eateries or other facilities in the modern sense, and meals were eaten in private; visitors either brought their own food to be prepared, or else a full board alternative would be provided.

Did you know?

The English use of the term hotel dates from 1765 and is a French contraction of the word hostel, denoting an inn, especially 'one of a superior kind'.

Despite being named as such, the hotel as a distinct and separate architectural phenomenon was yet to emerge, but at fashionable resorts accommodation was provided within assembly room complexes often resembling terraces or grand houses. They were a central part of social life, hosting functions and property auctions, as at Margate's Royal Hotel, Tavern and Assembly Rooms, built by 1794, and at Brighton the existing Old Ship Hotel added assembly rooms in 1767. In Weymouth entrepreneur Andrew Sproule built a hotel and assembly rooms in the 1770s; Stacie's Hotel (later the Royal Hotel) opened in 1773, and was one of the first purpose-built seaside hotels, with separate rooms for families and small groups and connecting dining rooms and bedrooms. Somewhat later, the neoclassical Royal Hotel, Plymouth, of 1819 was built as part of an impressive complex with a theatre and assembly rooms, and due to its absence of inn-like characteristics, it is regarded as the first luxury coastal hotel. Collonaded stables and coach houses ran along two sides of a large central courtyard and there was a main building range for public functions. Facilities included a Large Dining Room or Room for Assembly, a Commercial Room, Coffee Rooms and small dining rooms; separately accessed hotel accommodation comprised five en suite bedrooms, and private dining and sitting rooms on the two upper floors.

The Royal Hotel, Plymouth, by Llewellyn Frederick William Jewitt, dating from the mid-nineteenth century. Its architect was John Foulston, who won a competition in 1811 with his neo-Classical design, the height of architectural fashion. (©Victoria and Albert Museum, London)

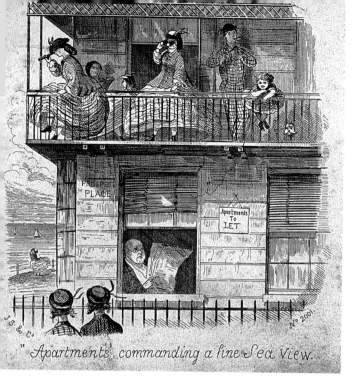

"Apartments commanding a fine Sea View."

Nineteenth-century wood engraving from *Sea-side Sketches*, published by F. Knott. (Wellcome Library no. 35192i)

As visitor numbers grew, a hierarchy of accommodation became increasingly evident, with a flourishing of cheap lodging houses, all-inclusive boarding houses and private hotels, and a very real need for exclusive accommodation. The costs of building entirely new premises could be high, so some enterprising individuals converted houses into bona fide hotels. In 1819 the first large-scale hotel in Brighton, boasting an impressive hundred beds, was formed from the conversion of three houses known as Steine Place by a Dr Hall, and was named the Royal Hotel after the Duke of York, brother of the Prince Regent. It soon became the town's most fashionable venue, holding balls, concerts and recitals in the public rooms.

Did you know?

Victorian grand hotel names were often chosen to lend an often spurious connection with royalty, and so there are abundant Royals and Imperials. Notable royal residences were also commemorated in later hotels, with names such as Palace and Carlton.

Resort architecture was increasingly influenced by factors other than pure function, stemming from a burgeoning interest in aesthetics, panoramas, nature, and sea views from the end of the eighteenth century. As attitudes and perceptions towards the coast changed, new buildings were designed to accommodate panoramas, especially sea views, seen in the sea-facing architecture of Regency resorts such as Brighton and Weymouth. Bournemouth's first purpose-built resort house, completed in 1812, was designed to have 'magnificent seaview prospects', the location being specifically chosen for its remote and attractive situation. The mansion and grounds were initially enjoyed as a summer residence by its builder, retired army officer Lewis Tregonwell and his wife Henrietta, but was being let as a holiday home to wealthy acquaintances by 1820.

The Tregonwell Mansion, Bournemouth, later the Royal Exeter Hotel. Built in 1812 as a 'holiday home' by Lewis Tregonwell when his wife Henrietta took a fancy to the area, it was later leased to gentry, including the Marchioness of Exeter, after whom it was later named.

This image of the Royal Exeter Hotel was reproduced on the reverse of playing cards for hotel guests. The hotel incorporates the Tregonwell Mansion, which, despite later extensions, can still be identified.

Large-scale enterprises began to emerge as the commercial potential for providing high-end seasonal accommodation was recognised. Exclusive planned speculative developments began to appear around the coast, invariably with an impressive hotel as the focal point, providing new and exclusive resorts for a wealthy clientele. In the 1790s a new resort at Southend was planned in the hope of establishing a new resort to rival Margate, Brighton and Weymouth. The first phase of the 'New Town' was formed by what became Nos 1–15 Royal Terrace and the Royal Hotel, but the development wasn't initially successful. At the western edge of Hastings renowned London developers James and Decimus Burton created a 'Regents Park by the Sea' between 1825 and 1835, an ambitious planned resort stretching for over half a mile along the coast that became St Leonards-on-Sea. The St Leonards Hotel was the dramatic focal point with pedimented double arched entrances and two tiers of giant Corinthian order, very much resembling a grand residence. The hotel's 'superior accommodation' with spacious rooms and magnificent interior was aimed at the nobility and their families and attracted an enviable clientele. The resort blossomed, especially following the patronage of the young Princess Victoria and her mother, who stayed in 1834, setting a royal precedent, and with permission the hotel was renamed the Royal Victoria Hotel following her accession to the throne.

St Leonards, 1834. St Leonards Hotel, now the Royal Victoria, was the focal point of the planned development. It opened in 1829 with a gala banquet for over 200 guests, fireworks, a huge bonfire and a grand ball. (Reproduced by permission of Hastings Museum and Art Gallery)

Other planned resorts were less flamboyant. In the 1830s landowner Sir George William Tapps-Gervis sought to create a genteel and exclusive estate resort at what is now Bournemouth, to the design of architect Benjamin Ferrey. A series of villas and two hotels, the Bath Hotel and the Bellevue Boarding House, were constructed from 1837–8. The exclusive character of the estate was successfully preserved for several decades, mostly because of its still-remote location, and growth was gradual until much later.

The exclusive purpose-built hotel was becoming a familiar and recognisable component of the coast, but within a few years a period of hotel building would ensue on a scale never before seen, both in terms of number and building size. The era of the grand hotel had arrived.

The original form of Bath Hotel, Bournemouth, was modest in concept, and unrecognisable from the sprawling and much extended Royal Bath Hotel of today.

2
The Growth of the Grandiose

The mid to late nineteenth century was the golden age of the grand seaside hotel, as a showpiece luxury establishment became a must-have for any successful resort; by the end of the Victorian era each seaside resort possessed at least one. This proliferation of grand hotel building occurred at the same time as the opening up of the coast from the 1840s by the expanding rail network, which provided an efficient and affordable conduit for a whole new set of visitors to the coast, all requiring accommodation. Existing resorts flourished and still more resorts were established as the coastline became increasingly accessible. Although most of the new influx of visitors used the numerous lodgings and guesthouses which remained the predominant source of accommodation, there was an enduring want and need for grander accommodation from the nobility and the wealthy middle classes. This coincided with the Joint Stock Companies Act of 1844, which enabled private enterprise to flourish, and entrepreneurs keen to exploit the new market established companies specifically to raise the necessary funds to build new hotels at potentially successful locations.

The planned resort continued to be significant in seaside development, and the presence of a grand hotel was crucial for attracting wealthy visitors, and therefore revenue. The reasons for location choice varied, and remote locations continued to be popular, preceding or coinciding with the arrival of the railway. In 1846 surveyor Owen Williams developed plans to transform the marshland behind Llandudno Bay into an elegant resort and presented them to John Williams, agent of landowner Lord Mostyn. The scheme was approved and designs included the prominent seaward-facing St George's Hotel, built for local publican

St George's Hotel, Llandudno. The original building was later extended along St George's Place to create extra accommodation as the resort grew in popularity. (Brian Clift)

Isaiah Davies, who allegedly acquired the prime site by cancelling Williams' drinking debts. The hotel opened in 1854, and remained one of the town's most prestigious hotels, attracting high-status guests including Napoleon III and Empress Eugénie.

Sometimes the choice of location was for more unexpected reasons. Following the success of Charles Kingsley's novel *Westward Ho!*, published in 1855, the Northam Burrows Hotel & Villa Company was formed in 1863 to build an elegant self-contained exclusive resort at the hitherto isolated location. It comprised several villas centred around an imposing domestic Gothic-style hotel set within 75 acres. Thirty-three luxury bedrooms were provided and later a separate building to the east of the hotel was built to accommodate servants of the guests. Originally named the Royal Hotel, it was renamed Westward Ho! Hotel after Charles Kingsley accepted an invitation to attend the opening ceremony, but it later reverted to the Royal Hotel following the patronage of the Prince of Wales.

Elsewhere, locations for planned resorts complete with resplendent hotel were selected because of links between the speculative developer and the impending arrival of the railway. Lowestoft station opened following the incorporation of the Lowestoft Railway & Harbour Company in 1845 to build a harbour and dock railway. The scheme was promoted by entrepreneur and civil engineering contractor Samuel Morton Peto, who acquired nearby low-value farmland and commonland to establish a pleasure resort of terraces of grand townhouses overlooking the beach. The first phase stretched over half a mile along the seafront, including Marine Parade, Wellington Esplanade and Kirkley Cliff, and included the Royal Hotel at the north end of the Esplanade, built for successful hotelier Samuel Howett. Development continued with Marine Parade running parallel to the west of the Esplanade, with a second Howett hotel, the Harbour Inn, mirroring the Royal Hotel. Rather tellingly, an early distinction was made between the 'inferior' Marine Parade and the 'pretentious' Esplanade where the Royal was located.

The 1860s Westward Ho! Hotel, later renamed the Golden Bay Hotel, was extended in 1900 to accommodate tearooms, which were later converted to the Anchor Public House. The hotel commanded sweeping coastal views.

The extension of the railway line at Saltburn led into the North Eastern Railway's Zetland Hotel at the rear of the main station, seen here in 2016. (Hugh Llewelyn)

Cliff-top land at Saltburn was identified as a prospective seaside resort by railway owner Henry Pease. The Saltburn Improvement Company was formed and in 1861 a Parliamentary Bill enabled a branch railway line, sea-facing houses, and hotel to be constructed. The Zetland Hotel, designed by William Peachey, was an imposing monumental building, dominating the coastline with a distinctive cylindrical viewing tower facing the sea, and had fifty bedrooms. Located next to the train shed and private platform, it was one of the world's earliest railway hotels. Although Saltburn was never quite as successful a seaside resort as elsewhere, it remained popular enough for a second hotel to be built around 1871, the Coatham Victoria Hotel, designed by C. J. Adams.

Railway companies themselves gradually came to own several seaside hotels, mostly purpose-built, although, more rarely, they were acquired. The first hotel marketed by the Great Western Railway company as a destination hotel, rather than being a stop-off for travellers, was Tregenna Castle, St Ives, Cornwall, situated on a prime cliff-top location overlooking the bay. The Great Western Railway leased and converted the building into a hotel to broadly coincide with the opening in 1877 of the railway station directly below.

The railway was a catalyst for the building of many grand hotels at existing resorts, often built near to stations and accessed by covered walkways leading from the platforms to the hotel entrance. Other hotels had porters in attendance together with hotel-owned horse-drawn omnibuses to meet guests from trains. Very often, the arrival of the railway heralded a flurry of hotel building, abruptly and irrevocably altering the character of a resort both socially and architecturally. Bournemouth had remained a relatively small and exclusive

The Royal Bath Hotel, Bournemouth, was much enlarged *circa* 1880 in response to the town's rapid expansion as a resort. Its attractions included a Mikado Room, extensive grounds, tennis courts, an ornamental pond and views of the pier.

resort for wealthy visitors for some decades, but the arrival of the railway in 1870 changed this forever as the town boomed and a number of new hotels were built to accommodate the influx of holidaymakers. Existing hotels needed to rapidly expand to remain viable competitors and between 1878 and 1880 the Bath Hotel was extended and reconstructed at great cost, and renamed the Royal Bath Hotel.

Although architecturally there was no single grand hotel style, they exemplified a new form of seaside architecture by virtue of their sheer visual dominance and scale. These were buildings to be seen, with dominant locations specifically selected at seafront or cliff-top sites and monumental design to incorporate sweeping sea views. Integral interior opulence included sumptuously and often exotically themed and decorated ballrooms, restaurants, smoking rooms, baths and several waiting areas. The grand scale, magnitude and significance of these hotels attracted some of the era's most distinguished architects, entrepreneurs, and guests, and lavish opening ceremonies were invariably accompanied with pomp and ceremony.

The architectural form of these buildings was dictated by the needs of the hotel. Exclusivity was paramount, and monumentality, design and materials set these hotels apart from existing resort buildings, thereby marking them as select. Exclusion of those who did not belong was ensured not only by the cost of accommodation, but by their design: wide entrances, grand lobbies and décor were undoubtedly daunting for those deemed to have no place there, and where present, uniformed doormen were unquestionably an excellent deterrent. Furthermore, once inside, strict societal codes dictated dress and behaviour within specific public rooms.

Left: Advertisement for the new
Metropole Hotel, Brighton, 1890. Many
typical grand hotel attributes are depicted,
albeit exaggerated for publicity purposes:
monumental frontage, grand entrance,
opulent decor, grand staircase, imposing
purpose-specific rooms and delineated
spaces. (*Illustrated London News*, 26 July
1890)
Below: Detail of the restored interior,
Grand Hotel, Scarborough.

A large resident staff performing numerous specialist roles was needed to maintain the high standards of luxury required. The largest hotels typically employed a manager and sub-manager, with a head day porter, head night porter, and head housekeeper to manage female domestic staff. A superintendent often oversaw any public rooms such as the lounge and billiards room, and separate head waiters were required for the coffee room, the table d'hôte room, the ladies' room for family dining, and private banqueting rooms. A head cellarman curated the inevitably extensive wine stocks and spirits and a head plateman took charge of crockery and cutlery. An usher oversaw the servants' hall, and there were also staff for the linen, laundry and still rooms as well as chambermaids, porters, page boys, lift men and receptionists.

An efficient and well-run kitchen was essential to any grand hotel, especially as there were essentially three types of meals to prepare, for the guests, their servants, and the hotel servants, and the quality and range of food served was essential to a hotel's reputation. Within the kitchen clearly defined divisions of labour were represented by a head chef and several under chefs, usually a roast chef, sauce chef, pastry chef and cold larder chef, as well as associated apprentices, head kitchen maid, fish maid, head and under vegetable maid, one or two scrubber maids, kitchen porters, and washers-up. Guests' servants were usually looked after in the stewards' room, often below stairs, and were fed better than hotel staff. The children of guests would often eat there too with their nanny.

Grand hotels built at resorts all around the coast were typically large, dominant and luxurious, with countless examples, such as The Queens Hotel, Hastings (1862), The Palace Hotel, Southport (1866) and The Imperial Hotel, Blackpool (1867). The Ilfracombe Hotel, north Devon, is a particular lovely example of the era, with an ornate French Gothic exterior and effective use of polychromy. Built in 1867, it was the town's first purpose-built luxury seafront hotel, with 210 rooms and attic rooms for the guests' servants. Torquay's Imperial

Blackpool Imperial Hotel, opened 1867. Designed in a French Renaissance and Baroque style, its imposing red brick façade, stone dressings and wide entrance are characteristic of many Victorian grand hotels. Nikolaus Pevsner described it as the 'climax of Blackpool hôtelerie'. (Jack Deighton)

The Ilfracombe Hotel of 1867 was the town's first purpose-built luxury hotel and occupied a prominent prime seafront site. A classic French Gothic building, it had decorated lancet windows, a high pitched roof with dormer windows, and heavy buttressed chimneys.

Hotel of 1866 was a more lavish and luxurious establishment 'for gentlemen and families', with all fifty rooms facing the sea. Its cliff-top location overlooking Torbay was supposedly the finest on the English Riviera. Although perhaps spurious at some hotels, royal connections here were real, and were used to great marketing advantage. Guests included a large number of royal and European dignitaries, among them the Prince of Wales and the Queen of the Netherlands in 1870 and Napoleon III in 1871, and following his stay Prince Albert praised the hotel for being the perfect place for relaxation and recuperation. Royal connections were important in attracting and retaining an elite clientele. The small harbour town of North Berwick in Scotland received its grand hotel in 1875 with the building of the Marine Hotel. It attracted a distinguished summer clientele including Prince Edward of Saxe-Weimar and his wife, who travelled from their London home each year, popularising both the hotel and the town.

The epitome of the grand Victorian seaside hotel is unquestionably represented by the two monumental, elaborately designed and aptly named Grand Hotels at Brighton and at Scarborough, which had monumental and elaborate costs to match: Scarborough's Grand cost in excess of £100,000 and that at Brighton £150,000. Scarborough's Grand was designed by 'master of the grandiose' Cuthbert Brodrick and was located in a prime position at St Nicholas Cliff, overlooking South Bay. Its immense design was in part inspired by architecture on the French Côte d'Azur and was one of the first giant purpose-built hotels in Europe. It was an immense undertaking, occupying an awkward space and being partly set into the cliff face. Over 6 million bricks were utilised and ten storeys rose from beach level to roof. After two years, however, the money ran out and in 1865 the venture was sold to a new company. It was eventually completed in 1867, its opening marked with a lavish opening banquet and ball for 200 guests.

QUEEN'S HOTEL, HASTINGS.

Right: The Queen's Hotel, Hastings, was completed in 1862 and had three guest entrances: a grand front entrance, a covered side carriage entrance and one for families desiring privacy. This advertisement stressed its tram-free frontage.

Below: Imperial Hotel, Torquay. Opened in 1866, the luxury hotel had ensuite bedrooms and was so popular that it was extended in 1870. In 1912 a motor garage was built when the Imperial became the headquarters of Torquay's Royal Automobile Club.

The only First-Class Licensed Hotel facing the Sea in Hastings or St. Leonards where the Trams do not pass in front

E. HAROLD PAULL,
Manager.

Did you know?

The Grand Hotel, Scarborough, is widely regarded as having design elements incorporated around the theme of time: four towers representing the seasons, twelve floors for the months of the year, fifty-two chimneys symbolising weeks of the year, and 365 guest bedrooms, one for each day of the year... However, the real number of rooms was closer to 300.

The Brighton Hotel Company was established to construct the Grand Hotel on prime seafront land. It was an impressive building, and despite being a huge undertaking, standing at eight storeys with over 150 bedrooms, and equipped with all-modern features, luxurious décor and furnishings, it took just eighteen months to complete and was formally opened in 1864. It was luxuriously and opulently furnished and no expense was spared. Staggering quantities include the installation of five water-operated passenger lifts, 15 miles of wallpaper, 12 miles of bell wire, and 230 marble chimney pieces.

There were some exceptions to the overly ostentatious rule. Eastbourne was developed as a genteel resort from the 1850s 'for gentlemen by gentlemen' by its two main landowners, the Duke of Devonshire and John Davies Gilbert. Elegant terraces of hotels and shops were built over twenty years or so, including the vast Burlington Hotel at Grand Parade, which was extended to its current size after 1860 when it acquired the leases of the adjacent houses.

The imposing façade of The Grand, Brighton. (Sammyone/ Shutterstock.com)

The Burlington Hotel and Royal Parade, Eastbourne, viewed from the pier. The hotel, opened in 1851, was one of Eastbourne's most prestigious developments of the time. (Dave Webb)

It wasn't until 1871, however, that the town received its first truly grand hotel, the Cavendish. Built in the French Gothic style, it represented the pinnacle of the town's hotel building despite the arrival of the spectacular Grand Hotel in 1877.

Not all grand seaside hotels were grandly Gothic or overtly opulent. The Sandringham Hotel, Hunstanton, the Westward Ho! Hotel and the Valley of Rocks Hotel, Lynton, are all visibly more restrained in character, although with classic Victorian Gothic characteristics. A complete and early departure from the style is represented by the 1873 Boscombe Spa Hotel (later the Chine Hotel), designed by architect Robert William Edis for Sir Henry Drummond Wolff, an early example of his Queen Anne Revival work. With a naturally occurring spring and attractive landscape, Wolff hoped to rival the adjacent resort of Bournemouth, although it never quite became as populist. The hotel itself was subsequently extended several times to accommodate increasing guest numbers, which in later years included performers from the nearby Boscombe Hippodrome.

Not all of the era's grand hotels were purpose-built. As with the Tregenna Hotel, converting existing residences into hotels, especially those commanding prominent locations, often in what were then still relatively remote – and therefore exclusive – locations, was potentially lucrative. One of the earliest was the Castle House Hotel, Aberystwyth, an Early English-style building incorporating a picturesque three-sided house designed by John Nash in 1794. It was redeveloped in 1864 by railway entrepreneur Thomas Savin, who envisioned a grand hotel to accommodate the potentially large number of visitors the railway would bring to the area. Unfortunately, after spending £80,000, the hotel only partly opened, and Savin was bankrupted. It was purchased by the newly formed University College of Wales and was subsequently rebuilt for university premises. Elsewhere, conversions were more successful, including the Grand Hotel in Tynemouth, built as a summer residence in 1872 for the Duchess of Northumberland, but converted to a luxurious hotel in 1877; the Imperial Hotel, Llandudno, created in 1872 from merging several boarding houses; and the Norbreck Castle Hotel, Blackpool, built as a large country house in 1869 and bought by J. H. Shorrocks, who held lavish weekend parties there. Seeing financial potential, he began taking paying guests.

The Boscombe Spa Hotel was later renamed the Chine Hotel, and was much extended. The original Arts and Crafts structure can be seen at the centre.

Castle House Hotel, Aberystwyth, under construction in 1865. This shows the original south wing of the hotel, remodelled in the 1880s for the University College of Wales, which dominates today's seafront. (Reproduced by permission of Ceredigion Archives)

The somewhat incongruous Norbreck Castle Hotel, Blackpool. The hotel disco became a renowned gig venue in the late 1970s; bands included Angelic Upstarts, Penetration, a pre-famous Adam and the Ants, the Stray Cats and The Pretenders. (© Tricia Neal)

As seaside resorts became ever more established, with their abundant establishments offering accommodation of various standards and quality, from single rooms to elite hotels, it was increasingly necessary for hotels to advertise in local guidebooks and the press. Brochures and carte de visites, early versions of the picture postcard, were given to guests as advertisements and mementos. At several of the popular resorts such as Torquay, Brighton and Bournemouth with more than one luxury establishment, it was necessary for hotels to publicise their unique selling points. Scarborough's Grand emphasised its sophistication as being managed along the lines of 'many new American models', and the Grand in Brighton had a ventilation system using air displacement and lifts or 'rising rooms'. Proximity to the local station was important, and also to sea bathing premises if not part of the hotel's facilities. A hotel's location at a place of natural beauty or interest continued to be an attraction, whether explored by foot or viewed from the hotel, and gentle pursuits such as walking or tennis were also deemed desirable. At Lynton, the Valley of the Rocks Hotel was 'situated in its own Magnificent Grounds 600 feet above and facing the sea' and the Ilfracombe Hotel promoted its 5 acres of ornamental grounds and six lawn tennis courts.

Weather was important to the prosperity and profits of the grand seaside hotel and a good summer season was essential at many resorts to prevent profit slumps following a poor summer. Northern hotels in particular initially opened only for a short summer season; Scarborough's Grand opened during just July and August for some years, although resorts such as Torquay with milder climates fared much better, with a 'season' in place from October until Easter and many guests staying for several months. The lucrative winter market was soon more widely recognised, however, and hotels began acquiring innovative 'warming apparatus' for the colder months, thus lengthening their seasons and expanding their profits.

The emergence of the hydro hotel in the mid-nineteenth century influenced the introduction of the winter season at some coastal resorts, especially on the North West and Welsh coasts. Some way between a nursing home and a hotel, these usually extensive establishments used hydrotherapy and specialist baths to treat bronchial ailments, asthma and 'weakness of the vocal organs'. Their success was largely reliant upon the presence of medical professionals to add credibility, as was the custom of holiday guests as well as patients, and so facilities needed to appeal to both. Most seaside hydros were located at prominent seafront locations, offering winter heating alongside an impressive array of different baths and treatments. The prominent 'High class and up to date' Aberystwyth Hydro Hotel was particularly successful, with its hundred rooms,

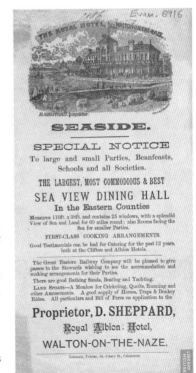

Advertisement for the Royal Albion Hotel, Walton-on-the-Naze, c. 1886. The location and sea views are emphasised, as are its impressive facilities, reflecting the perceived requirements of people visiting the seaside at this time. (British Library: Evan 6916)

Hydro-electric bath, 1892, from *The Hydro-Electric Methods in Medicine* by W. A. Hedley. (Wellcome Library)

radiator heating, and hot and cold sea baths supplied by sea water pumped into the hydro twice daily. A selection of medicated baths were available, and therapies including electric baths and high-frequency treatments were supervised by a qualified nurse. Further north, the Llandudno Hydropathic Establishment & Winter Residence was designed and built by Dr Edward Norton and was equipped with hydropathic appliances, four Russian vapour baths, two Turkish baths, a seaweed or ozone bath for rheumatism and a compressed air bath to facilitate easy breathing for asthmatics. Blackpool's Imperial Hydro also had an impressive variety of at least ten types of bath, including Russian, Sitz, needle, spray and rain, as well as the ubiquitous sea water.

By the 1870s and 1880s the success and reputation of the grand seaside hotel as a luxury establishment made them desirable assets, and established hoteliers and fledgling hotel groups began to cast their eyes coastward. The growth of the Gordon Hotels Company Ltd was largely due to the success of their London hotels, overseen by entrepreneurial hotelier and founder Frederick Gordon. In the 1880s Gordon had built, acquired and extended several significant seaside hotels, among them the Cliftonville Hotel, Margate; the Burlington, Eastbourne; and the Grand Hotel, Broadstairs. However, it was the construction of the Metropole Hotel in Brighton in 1890 that really consolidated their reputation at the coast. In an age where competition for retaining guests was ever-present, the construction of the vastly larger, grander and visually more striking Metropole Hotel practically next door to the existing Grand was a bold action.

The new hotel outshone its smaller, older neighbour in every way, not least as its architect was RIBA president Alfred Waterhouse, whose trademark red brick and terracotta contrasted greatly with the predominantly Regency stucco architecture of the seafront. There were 700 rooms including 340 bedrooms, and large and lavishly decorated public rooms included a library, smoking room, lounge, billiards room and famously extensive wine cellars holding 185,000 bottles. A dining area seating 500 could be divided into three by glass walls, and there were a series of luxurious baths. The hotel was furnished by Maple & Co., suppliers to aristocracy and royalty, with whom Gordons established a close business connection. The opening of the Metropole proved disastrous for the Grand, whose visitor numbers fell drastically as even loyal guests flocked to its more lavish and modern Metropole.

By the end of the nineteenth century the large and purpose-built, architect-designed grand hotel was established as an essential component of the seaside resort, having contributed to the latter's growth in size, wealth and importance. They provided luxury and sumptuous accommodation for the wealthy middle classes and for the nobility, and this would continue, at least while some seaside resorts retained their genteel and exclusive character.

The magnificent polished marble staircase with alabaster balusters, Metropole, Brighton. The hotel's other major marble feature was a chimneypiece carved by Prince Victor of Hohenlohe-Langenburg, nephew of Queen Victoria, which was removed in the 1960s. (Jay Garrett)

Rival Brighton hotels The Metropole and The Grand.

Italian Garden, Metropole Hotel, Brighton. The attractive terraced Italian Garden flanked the Clarence Rooms on two sides, but was built over by conference rooms in the 1960s.

3
Flourishing Flamboyance and the End of an Era

By the end of the nineteenth century and start of the twentieth, most seaside resorts were fully established and the era of the opulent grand seaside hotel was still in full swing. In many ways this was the last great era of hotel building for a truly elite clientele, as in subsequent periods both new and existing grand hotels became more accessible and affordable for a wider spectrum of people. As before, when newer seaside resorts began to blossom, grand hotels were soon built, although fashionable architectural styles had shifted. As the last monumental hotels in the 'grand tradition' were completed, there emerged statement showy Edwardian seaside hotels, reminiscent of buildings along the French and Italian rivieras and Mediterranean coastline. Many continued to be named Grand, and those built by Gordon Hotels were regularly called Metropole. Hotels of this period were often sited at commanding locations, often on cliff tops, and of course were fully equipped with all modern conveniences, including electric lighting and heating throughout.

The building of hotels at existing resorts continued, sometimes on the site of existing structures at prime locations. In 1900 the striking Metropole Hotel, Blackpool, was the result of a drastic remodelling of the former eighteenth-century Bailey's Hotel, which doubled its size. Eclectic and lavish interiors included suites as well as bedrooms, and a Moorish-style lounge, a Louis XV-style drawing room and a Georgian-style dining room. The attractive red brick Royal Hotel, Weymouth, completed in 1899, was also rebuilt on the site of an earlier eighteenth-century hotel, demolished eight years earlier. Its significant seafront location and Queens Ballroom to the rear ensured an immediate and lasting popularity. In 1902 an existing hotel and bathhouse at Llandudno's North Shore were transformed into the new Grand Hotel, the largest in Wales at that time with 158 rooms.

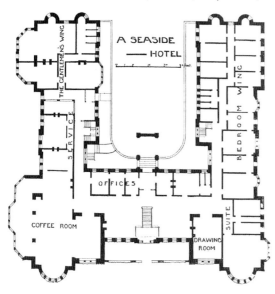

'A Seaside Hotel' in Cornwall, 1898. This Bude hotel had all the expected attributes of the era: a cliff-top location, the usual public rooms, ensuite bedrooms and basement service rooms. Interestingly, all façades were designed as a front elevation. (*The Builder*, 16 July 1898)

Metropole Hotel, Blackpool. Its enviable and unequalled position on the shoreline is due to its construction on the site of the earlier eighteenth-century Bailey's Hotel.

The Grand Hotel, Llandudno. A typical Edwardian grand hotel, key features are its dominant position, six storeys, and pyramidal roofs and tower. It was acquired by Butlins in 1981, and has since changed hands several times. (Wozzie/Shutterstock.com)

Empire Hotel, Lowestoft. Its life as a luxury hotel was sadly short-lived; following wartime requisitioning, it became St Luke's TB Hospital in 1922, which closed c. 1955. The building was demolished in 1958.

Among the last hotels to be built in the truly grand tradition were those in Lowestoft and Folkestone. At Folkestone, the imposing grandiose Metropole of 1897 and Grand of 1899 were built at the western end of The Leas as part of major development along the seafront. Gordon Hotels had secured the building contract for the Metropole but its isolated location facing the channel was compromised by the building of the adjacent Grand by local builder Daniel Baker, who, piqued at losing the Metropole contract, planned a larger, more impressive establishment. Baker implemented several building innovations, including waterproof cavity wall insulation, steel framing infilled with reinforced concrete, and suspended ceilings for improved soundproofing. As a 'gentlemen's residential chambers', the hotel immediately attracted an illustrious clientele, including regular visitor Edward VII. At Lowestoft the imposing Empire Hotel on Kirkley Cliff was built in 1900 by caterers and hoteliers Spiers & Pond Ltd, and with 200 bedrooms was the largest seaside hotel in Britain of the time. Facilities were modern and fashionable, including electric lighting, lifts to all floors, a library and several restaurants.

Developing resorts continued to be prime locations for new grand hotels built in new fashionable architectural styles. In the 1890s the French chateau-esque Grand, Metropole and Hotel de Paris, Cromer, were all built in dominant positions overlooking the sea. The Metropole was part of the Gordon Group, and in 1900 they added a western wing, itself large enough to be a substantial seaside hotel, with a hundred rooms to accommodate 150 guests. The Grand Hotel, Southwold, was built in 1901 as part of the northward expansion of the town by the Coast Development Company. Costing £30,000, the hundred-room hotel was modern through and through, with a lift to all floors, electric lights and central heating, and was luxuriously furnished by fashionable London suppliers James Shoolbred & Co. Set within extensive grounds of 3 acres, guests could arrive by rail and travel to the hotel without necessarily entering the town itself, and once there were provided with ample facilities including tennis courts and exotic gardens, ensuring there was no reason to leave.

An aerial view of Cromer's seafront and pier, showing the central and dominant position of the Hotel de Paris, its turrets and cupolas providing a dramatic skyline. The building replaced an earlier hotel of 1830, which was incorporated with adjacent properties into the new design. (John Fielding)

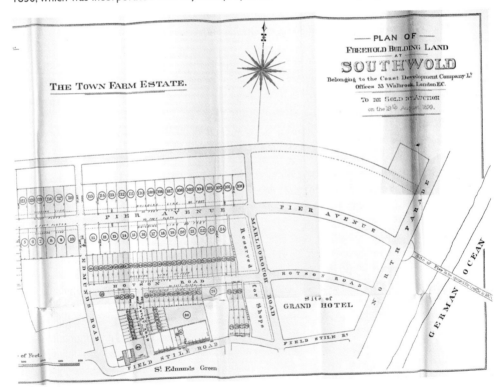

Plan of the Town Farm Estate, Southwold, 1899. The plan shows the plot of the proposed Grand Hotel to the south-east, a large and dominant building fronting North Parade. (Reproduced by permission of Suffolk Record Office, Lowestoft)

Headland Hotel, Newquay, Cornwall. The Grade II listed hotel opened in 1900 and commands a prominent position overlooking Fistral Beach and Towan Head. (Daniel Goodchild/Shutterstock.com)

The Headland Hotel, Newquay, Cornwall, completed in 1900, was an especially opulent and luxurious masterpiece, designed by Cornish architect Silvanus Trevail. Its rooms were lavishly decorated and facilities included hot and cold running water, electric lights, state of the art service bells, and the all-important magnificent sea views. The hotel retained its elite status for many years and attracted a host of wealthy and illustrious guests, notably Edward VII and Queen Alexandra, the first of many royals to stay there.

Less ostentatious hotels include the Grand, Swanage, of 1898, which, although not so grandiose in concept, and more stylistically akin to the earlier Boscombe Spa Hotel, was set apart by its location away from the older town and its commanding view overlooking the bay. The relatively remote situations of many hotels of this era were perfectly suited to be associated with golf links, increasingly popular from this time. Several hotels were specifically marketed for golfing pursuits, often incorporating 'golf' or 'links' into their names, as did the Golf View Hotel, Nairn, opened in 1897, and the Links Hotel, Skegness. Links were also established at Ravenscar in 1898 by the Earl of Cranbrooke, associated with the Ravenscar Hotel, opened in 1897 by the Peak Hall Estate Company as part of plans to establish a rival resort to nearby Scarborough.

Many existing hotels were modernised and redeveloped to compete with their newer counterparts. In 1891 the Scarborough Hydro was extended at a cost of £25,000 for 120 additional bedrooms, a grand floral hall and other public rooms, and by 1903 the Ilfracombe Hotel had electricity installed throughout the building and grounds, which were dramatically illuminated by night. The Pavilion Hotel, Folkestone, underwent a major refurbishment and rebuilding in 1899 and in 1903 the interior of the Royal Victoria Hotel at St Leonards was remodelled.

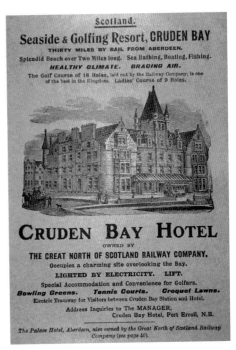

Above left: The Grand Hotel, Swanage. The front of the hotel has been much altered, although some original features remain. The rear of the building shows the original symmetry, and it is this façade that faces the bay, and which can be seen from the town. (Jay Garrett)

Above right: Advertisement for the Cruden Bay Hotel, 1908. The Great North of Scotland Railway Company promoted this new seaside and golfing resort, which had the hotel at its centre.

Below: Raven Hall Hotel, Ravenscar. In the 1890s it was converted from the mid-eighteenth-century Peak Hall when the Peak Hall Estate was transformed into a holiday resort. In 1897 the village name was changed from Peak to Ravenscar. (© Adam Kerfoot-Roberts)

At many resorts, establishing new hotels was clearly still deemed potentially lucrative, and as in previous decades, a significant number of grand hotels were created by converting existing residences, usually purchased by entrepreneurs or companies seeking to capitalise on seaside tourism. In Paignton, Devon, the Redcliffe Hotel was opened in 1903 following conversion of the Indian-inspired Gothic residence of retired engineer and contractor Robert Smith, and in Eastbourne, York House Hotel was established in 1896 by Susannah Barratt and her daughter Sarah, who acquired and extended houses along the Royal Parade terrace, built in 1883, between 1896 and 1938. In Torquay the former grand residence Villa Syracusa, which had been used as a convalescent home for Boer War casualties until 1901, was opened as the luxurious Torquay Hydro.

Times were rapidly changing, however, and by the early twentieth century most seaside towns were practically fully formed and were attracting hordes of people from all walks of life as family holidays became increasingly affordable and en-masse factory day trips became common. Resorts such as Blackpool, Great Yarmouth and Bournemouth rapidly lost their appeal among the higher echelons of society and grand hotels began losing their clientele as the gentry took their custom to quieter and often adjacent locations, such as St Annes from Blackpool, and Gorleston from Great Yarmouth. Some resorts sought to preserve exclusivity,

Torquay Hydro Hotel. The hotel capitalised on its isolated and exclusive location, proclaiming that it was 'world famous for its quiet dignity and efficiency [providing] that delightful atmosphere of tone which embraces artistic surroundings and the connoisseurs need'.

The Redcliffe Hotel, Paignton. When it opened in 1902 it was promoted as 'The Finest Health Resort in Devon,' and provided luxurious accommodation with opulent eastern-inspired furnishings, in keeping with its architecture.

as at Folkestone, when the newly built Metropole Hotel wanted to block general public access to the Leas; this was unsuccessful.

Changes in seaside holidays and accommodation requirements were influenced by the growth in popularity of the motor car and improvements to road networks, and hotels became more accessible and less exclusive. A new type of holiday began to emerge that demanded a new type of hotel, and motor garages and petrol began to be included in facilities offered to guests. By 1910 many of the earlier and now old-fashioned grand seaside hotels were beginning to decline in popularity. A few new large hotels were built, including the Walpole Bay Hotel, Margate, in 1914, which aimed to attract discerning guests, and Blackpool in particular experienced a spate of large hotels being built along the Promenade. However, the next decade was not a happy one for new and old hotels alike, and although pretty catastrophic for the hotel industry generally, for the grand seaside hotel it was especially challenging.

Above: Garage accommodation, Imperial Hotel, Hythe, *circa* 1910. Garages became an essential component of every hotel as the motor car came to replace the traditional horse and cart.

Left: Advertisement for Kings Hotel, Brighton. The usual attractions feature, with heating and sea views, etc., but perhaps uniquely there was also a poultry farm.

4
Twentieth-Century Troubles and Triumphs

The First World War had far-reaching and immediate consequences for the hotel industry. Tourism dwindled, staff enlisted and both staff and guests classed as enemy nationals left the country. The coast was also vulnerable to enemy attack and air raids along the South and East coasts in particular resulted in many direct hits. As early as December 1914, Scarborough was bombarded by the German navy, which resulted in a direct hit on the Grand Hotel. Fortunately, few guests were in residence and no-one was injured, but the damage was significant with repairs estimated at around £10,000.

Damage inflicted by the requisitioning of hotels proved more far-reaching, as hotels were commandeered for use as hospitals when hospitals were unable to cope with the volume of war wounded, and for wholesale use by government departments. The Empire Hotel, Lowestoft, was converted into a hospital for troops, and many others including The Grand, Broadstairs, and the Metropole, Folkestone, were requisitioned for army accommodation.

Requisitioned hotels had to find storage for furniture and furnishings, and prepare inventories, while those who managed to remain open were severely affected by rising costs of staff wages and items such as linen, glass, china and cutlery, as well as food costs and rationing. Restrictions by the Liquor Control Board on the sale of wines and spirits were placed on almost all English hotels as shortages took hold, resulting in reductions to the opening hours and the strength of spirits and liquors and beers.

Bomb damage at the Grand Restaurant, Grand Hotel, Scarborough, December 1914. Two shells hit the restaurant, and a third-floor bedroom was destroyed by a direct hit, with minor damage elsewhere. (World War One Photos Archive. www. WW1Photos.com)

Ilfracombe Museum occupies the former laundry building of the Ilfracombe Hotel, and as such is the hotel's sole surviving element. (Reproduced by permission of Ilfracombe Museum)

When the war ended the situation did not improve for many seaside hotels, which were hindered by the effects of inflation and not helped by non-returning staff and the need for refurbishment of buildings that were often already over fifty years old. Recovery was simply not possible in many cases, and buildings fell into disrepair or were unable to reopen. Lowestoft's Empire Hotel was acquired by the Metropolitan Asylum Board and used as a sanatorium from 1921, and part of the now run-down Ilfracombe Hotel was leased to the Council at the end of the 1920s and was refurbished as offices. In 1932 the hotel's former laundry was converted into the town's museum, leaving the remaining portion of the hotel to struggle on.

Trends in seaside holidays in place before the war continued to affect the larger seaside hotels, who found it difficult to compete with smaller, cheaper privately run hotels offering perfectly acceptable full board accommodation, together with the loss of custom from wealthier families who no longer visited the more popular resorts. Fortunately for those that managed to stay open, there was a general country-wide recovery in the early 1920s, a return of visitors from Europe, and the seaside holiday resumed, especially in the traditional resorts of Blackpool, Bournemouth and Scarborough as British seaside resorts were developed as tourist destinations. New grand hotels were built at these resorts, including Georgian revival and Baroque designed buildings. Seaside holidays were hugely bolstered by major advertising campaigns by the main railway companies, whose posters promoted rail travel to various destinations, often featuring specific destination hotels under their management.

Above: A postcard showing various views of the exterior and interior of the Cliffs Hotel, Blackpool. Built in 1921 to a Baroque design, with red brick and yellow terracotta, it remains a striking building on Queen's Promenade at the North Shore.

Right: Felixstowe's Felix Hotel featured as a somewhat looming Gothic edifice in this unusual railway poster when it reopened in 1925. It closed in 1950 or 1951 and is now apartments. (Reproduced by permission of the National Railway Museum)

W̦hy, there's Sam! Remember his wedding?

RATHER — WHEN THEY TOOK THE LABELS OFF HIS SUITCASES AND WROTE "BRITAIN'S MOST BEAUTIFUL GUEST HOUSE" ACROSS 'EM. . . .

Singularly appropriate, but rather cruel. . . .

CRUEL BE HANGED! EVERYTHING ARRIVED ALL RIGHT. WHERE ELSE COULD THEY GET TO?

I suppose, if you put it like that, the Palace was the only place to—

AND THE ONLY PLACE WHERE GOLF, TENNIS, CROQUET, BOWLS, SQUASH, BADMINTON, SWIMMING POOL, DANCING, CINEMA & ENTERTAINMENTS ARE ALL INCLUDED IN THE TERMS!

Just listen to him, Daphne, he knows it off by heart.

PALACE Hotel, TORQUAY

Britain's Most Beautiful Guest House

Left: In a departure from the usual advertorial format for extolling a hotel's virtues, the Palace Hotel, Torquay, used humour in this advertising campaign and ran several adverts along similar lines.
Below: Ocean Hotel, Saltdean, shortly after opening. The hotel was the epitome of modernity, offering an American Bar, first-class cuisine, exercise, pool and sunbathing facilities, hairdressing salons and a ballroom with 'the finest sprung floor in Britain'.

Social changes too influenced the hotel industry; this was a carefree time socially, and dinner, dancing and cabaret became popular as the trend for later nights took hold. Leisure time during a hotel stay very much revolved around the hotel itself; eating at other establishments was still relatively rare. This period also saw the opening up of hotel facilities to non-residents, a growing and lucrative market. Some of the older hotels modernised accordingly, as did the Grand Hotel, Southwold, which built a new recreation room for billiards and table tennis as well as introducing a cocktail bar and solarium open to non-residents. It also had garage accommodation, which was essential in an age when motor car ownership was higher than it had ever been.

The hotels of the English Riviera in particular enjoyed a thriving and buoyant period, and several new large high-end hotels were established by converting existing properties, so much altered that it was impossible to tell that they were not purpose-built. In 1925 Stearfield House, a grand residence built in 1870 and set within substantial grounds on Paignton's seafront, was acquired and extended to form the successful high-end Palace Hotel. In Torquay the Palace Hotel opened in 1921, successfully converted by newly retired Birmingham industrialist George W. Hands from a grand Italianate residence set in extensive grounds known as Bishopstowe, built in 1841 for the Bishop of Exeter. The hotel soon became renowned for its high standard of accommodation and abundant facilities included a golf course and covered swimming pool. A few years later in 1931 a row of Victorian houses known as Abbey Crescent occupying a prime Torquay seafront location was transformed to form the Art Deco Palm Court Hotel. The hotel was instantly popular, especially for its nightlife, and its in-house orchestra were often featured on the radio.

The Ballroom, Palace Hotel, Torquay.

The Palace Hotel, Paignton, occupies a prime seafront location, with sea-facing views. It was converted from the former home of Washington Singer, son of Isaac, founder of the Singer Sewing Machine Company.

Modernist Art Deco hotels dominated new seaside hotel building in the inter-war period. Although largely aimed at a classier clientele, they were relatively affordable to more people than in previous eras and offered a modern nightlife and lifestyle not always accessible in people's home lives. The iconic Midland Hotel, built in 1933, particularly exemplifies this new style of hotel. It was built for the London, Midland & Scottish Railway in a Streamline Moderne style to the designs of architect Oliver Hill and incorporated the period's fashionable design elements. Its curved design followed the line of the coast with large, sweeping sea-facing balconies, and there was a solarium for sunbathing at the top of a circular tower, reached by a spectacular central staircase illuminated at night through double glazed panels.

Did you know?

Despite appearing to be made of concrete, the modernist Midland Hotel at Morecambe was mainly constructed of bricks rendered with 'snowcrete', a mixture of white cement and carborundum.

The equally magnificent Art Deco Ocean Hotel at Saltdean near Brighton was built in 1938 and was set within 4 acres. It contained an impressive 334 bedrooms, 130 of these in the main curved building, and the rest within six detached blocks, which were closed in the winter. Facilities were modern, with the public rooms in the main building and an outdoor swimming pool (later enclosed) between the buildings. The Riviera Hotel, Bowleaze Cove, Dorset, of 1937 was another outstanding architectural masterpiece. Designed by L. Stewart Smith, it was constructed of reinforced concrete at an estimated cost of £40,000 and featured a host of classic Art Deco features including a central tower, picturesque archways and open air walkways.

Two Art Deco hotels in Bournemouth, The Cumberland Hotel, and the nine-storey Palace Court, were built between 1935 and 1937. The Palace Court was a classic Art Deco liner-style building, with wrap round curved suntrap balconies, a palmed garden, modern lounges and a cocktail bar. Unusually, there was direct access from the foyer to several shops, including a hairdresser, costumier and outfitter, and the upper storeys featured self-contained serviced flats. The ultra-modern Queen's Hotel in Torquay opened in 1937 and was stylistically similar to the Palace Court, although curiously the interior was traditionally furnished in heavy oak and teak. Classic 1930s facilities were provided, however, including a rooftop sun lounge and sun deck.

Above right: Seahorses and staircase, Midland Hotel, Morecambe. Several integral art pieces by Eric Gill include two Portland stone seahorses carved in situ for the entrance, modelled on Morecambe shrimp, and a circular plaster relief on the staircase ceiling. (Chris Coates, Morecambe)

Below: The Cumberland Hotel, Bournemouth, is a classic Art Deco designed building. When it opened, it offered a host of modern facilities, including 'English and Continental Cooking', showerbaths, 'scientific air conditioning' and telephones in all bedrooms.

Did you know?

In 1963 The Beatles stayed at the Palace Court Hotel, Bournemouth, where their iconic half-shadow image for the album cover of *With the Beatles* was shot, in a makeshift photo shoot in the hotel dining room.

Several Art Deco hotels built on a smaller scale were dominant within their landscapes, such as the Manchester Hotel in Blackpool, rebuilt in 1936 as a streamlined modernist building with an equally streamlined showpiece Art Deco bar; the Cavendish Hotel, Felixstowe; and the Grand, Sandown, on the Isle of Wight. One of the last seaside Art Deco hotels to be built was the Park Hotel in Tynemouth, designed by local architect J. R. Wallace and completed in 1939. With just thirty bedrooms and two suites, it was small but exclusive, and facilities included a ballroom that was popular for some years.

This golden inter-war period ended abruptly in 1939 with the onslaught of the Second World War, which proved more catastrophic for seaside hotels than the First had been as beaches were closed and mined and many resorts were heavily bombed, especially along the South Coast.

For some hotels it was initially business as usual for a time. Eastbourne's Grand Hotel flourished during 1940 with an abundance of visitors, and continued with its Christmas programme of 'variety and charm', including its annual children's fancy dress dance. Other Eastbourne hotels were less fortunate and many closed in 1940 for the duration of the war. Bombing raids of June 1941 damaged The Albion, Albermarle and York House hotels, and elsewhere damaged hotels included the Hydro Hotel in Falmouth, Cornwall.

The Montagu Park Hotel, Tynemouth, completed as the Park Hotel in 1939, was designed by local architect J. R. Wallace. Although smaller in scale than many of its Art Deco contemporaries, it is dominant within its own seaside landscape. (Kathleen and Allan Garrett)

The Luftwaffe bombing of the Metropole Hotel, Bournemouth, on 23 May 1943 killed almost 200 people staying at the hotel, mostly Allied airmen. (Reproduced by kind permission of Roger Shore, www.jp137.com61, original photograph from John Goslin)

As in the First World War, the biggest impact on the hotel industry was requisitioning, and countless seaside hotels were taken over by various government and military bodies. With its preponderance of hotels, Torquay was chosen to provide extensive training facilities and accommodation for the RAF, including The Grand, whose restaurant was used as a dormitory for trainees, and the Palace Hotel, which was used as a hospital. This proved damning as an enemy 'hit and run' campaign was launched against seaside hotels known to house RAF trainee aircrew and hospitals. On 25 October 1942 the Palace received a direct hit on the east wing, killing sixty-five patients and staff, and was evacuated to Wroughton the next day.

The US military were assigned to several hotels, among them the Royal Hotel, Weymouth, and Hydro Hotel, Falmouth (later the Royal Duchy Hotel), and the already beleaguered Ilfracombe Hotel was requisitioned by the Royal Army Pay Corps for offices and accommodation, with the tennis court being converted to a parade ground. The Marlborough Hotel, Cromer, was used by the Army, and Saltdean's Ocean Hotel was taken over by the Auxiliary Fire Service and was retained as a fire service college until 1952. The Grand at Sandown was central to PLUTO operations, acting as the control room for the supply mission during the D-Day landings.

Wales's seaside hotels were particularly affected as government departments were relocated from London to presumed greater safety. Practically all hotels in Llandudno and Colwyn Bay were impacted, the former by the vast Inland Revenue department relocating to the Imperial Hotel in spring 1940 and the requisitioning of over 400 hotels, boarding houses and private residences to accommodate department staff and families, while the Ministry of Food was assigned to the establishments of Colwyn Bay, notably the Metropole.

After the war seaside resorts took some time to recover as the beaches gradually opened again. New hotels were not really constructed for some years, and many existing grand hotels didn't reopen and were put up for sale, including the Imperial Hotel, Hythe, in 1946 and the Great Orme Hotel, Llandudno, in 1949. Others were more fortunate, reopening soon after the war ended, and in time visitor numbers steadily rose again as holiday seasons grew longer, although the clientele had perhaps changed in character from preceding decades.

DUE FOR DEMOB.
[1500 hotels requisitioned by the Government are to be released by the end of February, 1946]

Above left: This *Punch* cartoon by Leslie Illingworth from 1946 perfectly illustrates the sentiment of many hotels on their impending release from requisitioning following a gruelling few years of military and Government use. (© Punch Limited)

Above right: Guest Book page, Royal Hotel, Llandudno, June 1946. More affordable hotels were usually quicker to bounce back post-war; in June 1946 visitors came from diverse locations including London, Chobham and Sheffield. (Reproduced by permission from Conwy Archives)

Holidaying abroad was still affordable only to the wealthy and the recent introduction of annual paid leave allowed many working-class people to take holidays for the first time. Although the seaside holiday grew in popularity, most holidaymakers flocked to the increasingly popular holiday camps and caravan parks.

Conversely, holiday camps helped to resurrect some grand hotels. Butlins saw merit in providing hotel accommodation in large statement hotels and several sites were acquired, including five in Cliftonville, Margate, and the run-down Ocean Hotel at Saltdean in 1952. Following refurbishment, it opened as a holiday centre in May 1953 and proved to be a lucrative investment.

Generally though, independent grand hotels struggled to retain guests in an ever-changing sector. Guest expectations were higher, especially from overseas visitors used to private bathrooms, efficient in-bedroom heating and high-quality meals. Installation of central heating was difficult and expensive due to the solidity of these buildings and inadequate and badly situated kitchens designed in the previous century badly needed modernisation. Many hotels were unable to fulfil expectations, either due to unwillingness or inability to invest in refurbishment, and coupled with lingering post-war shortages and an inability to recover from being requisitioned, there were reductions in guest capacity and many hotels became even more run-down.

Above: A gaily painted Butlins hotel at Cliftonville, one of several Butlins resort hotels acquired in the 1950s. (Reproduced by permission from the John Hinde Archive)
Right: The only physical survival of the Hotel Metropole, Cromer, is a metal gate at the east end of the hotel site, bearing the initials HM. (Clive Lloyd)

The old-fashioned and ageing Victorian and Edwardian seaside hotels were particularly vulnerable to changes in popular taste and economics, and many fell into a semi-derelict state and were closed forever, among them Southwold's Grand, demolished in 1959 and replaced with bungalows, and Cromer's Metropole Hotel in 1955, which was replaced with flats. Other hotels faced conversion, as was the fate of the Westward Ho! Hotel; in 1963 its land was sold and the building was converted into fourteen flats.

Declining standards continued into the 1960s and were accompanied by a lack of confidence in building new hotels at the seaside. New hotels tended to be conversions of large Victorian houses or terraces knocked together, and existing grand hotels continued to struggle. The emergence of the chain hotel in this period was significant, and grand seaside hotels began to be acquired by large companies, becoming part of acquisitions and sales in subsequent decades, depending on economic fortunes. In the 1960s two major groups came to dominate the hotel industry: Grand Metropolitan and Trust House Hotels. They garnered the popular clientele as well as becoming popular with the corporate sector, providing catering and other leisure activities for conferences and events. By 1962 Trust House Hotels' seaside establishments included the Royal Victoria Hotel at St Leonards-on-Sea, the Metropole Hotel in Padstow and the Royal Albion Hotel in Broadstairs.

A sudden resurgence in hotel building followed the introduction of a Government Hotel Development Investment Scheme in 1968 that offered grants of £1,000 per bedroom for hotels built before 1973, and additional funds for extensions. The subsidies enabled hotel chains in particular to build new hotels with uniform standards and amenities and they tended to be boxy, practical, modern, functional and soulless, built at minimum cost to obtain maximum profit. There was no opulence or grandeur, and public rooms were generally replaced with profit-making conference and banqueting facilities, with minimal shared space, other than functional dining areas and lobbies. One of the only things in common with large seaside hotels of previous eras was the necessity for a hotel to have as many bedrooms as possible with sea views.

CAVENDISH HOTEL

Many hotel interiors refurbished at this time reflect fashionable style trends of the period; Eastbourne's Cavendish was no exception. The décor fits well with the modern, square hotel wing that replaced the original destroyed during the Second World War.

Right: The Manchester Hotel, Blackpool, in the 1970s. The hotel underwent alterations in the 1960s, although the exterior modernisation was not out of keeping with its 1930s design. (Ian McLoughlin, Blackpool)

Below: In 1977 the near-derelict 1930s Art Deco Saunton Sands Hotel was bought by Brend Hotels, who undertook a complete refurbishment. The hotel today comprises apartments and suites as well as rooms, many of them sea-facing. (John Fielding)

By the late 1970s there were over twenty hotel groups in Britain, including The Holiday Inn, Brend Hotels and Britannia Hotels, established in 1976. Many run-down hotels were acquired and refurbished, such as the expansive 1930s Art Deco Saunton Sands Hotel in Devon, bought and refurbished in 1977 by Brend Hotels. An excess of hotels with hundreds of rooms meant that competition was fiercer than ever before, especially as changes in holiday habits were beginning to take their toll on the popularity of Britain's seaside resorts as low-cost package holidays abroad in guaranteed sunshine began to take hold.

Did you know?

One of the conditions of sale for the purchase of the Royal Duchy Hotel, Falmouth, by the Brend Hotel Group in 1977 apparently stipulated that the grandfather clock in the cocktail bar had to be retained in the same position it had occupied for decades.

Some vast holiday hotels of this period include the remodelled Imperial Hotel, Torquay, which retained an opulent interior, but a completely transformed exterior makes it unrecognisable as the same hotel. In 1973–4 a curious transformation of the Royal Pavilion Hotel in Folkestone was undertaken by Motyl Burstin, who had apparently stayed at the hotel in the 1930s. The original 1843 hotel building was part-demolished and a bulky hotel resembling part of an ocean liner was built in the former hotel gardens, adjacent to the old hotel. In 1981–2 Burstin demolished most of the remaining Victorian building and extended the new structure to its current form.

The rebuilt Imperial Hotel, Torquay, is unrecognisable from its original incarnation.

The remodelled 'Burstin Motel', as Folkestone's Royal Pavilion was known, after its 1980s extension. The initial phase of rebuilding had left much of the original hotel building intact, although the old and the new looked rather incongruous side by side. (© Geoff Delivett)

The concept of the weekend and short break really took hold in this period, and a successful business model developed that remains current today, marketing to a weekend leisure clientele and a business clientele during the week. The decline in many resorts had consequences for all seaside accommodation, but the grand hotels remained the hardest hit, especially as affordability was a major factor. To compete with their modern counterparts, many were

The Queens Hotel has 100 bedrooms, many with private bathrooms. We can offer every possible facility from bars to comfortable lounges. The Queens is situated close to shopping, entertainment including the pleasure beach and the South Pier. During the season we offer entertainment in the hotel. We do hope we have the pleasure to serve you when next you visit Blackpool — THE RESORT.

A brochure for the Queen's Hotel, Blackpool, from the early 1980s. Some seaside hotels still preferred to target the non-budget, adult market, and promoted a classier experience.

reduced to lowering standards and prices to attract custom, such as the Grand, Scarborough, and many Blackpool hotels; the cost of staying at such establishments may have been affordable to many more people than ever before, but luxurious accommodation it was not.

By the 1990s most grand hotels were not attracting enough custom to remain viable, and even some hotel chains were clearly struggling. In 1990 the Trust House chain, as Forte Hotels, was broken up and its many hotels sold off. Many grand hotels became severely run down and closed or continued to struggle.

The author enjoying dinner at a grand Blackpool hotel, 1977. Many hotels such as this one began lowering prices and welcoming private coach trip parties. Although often appealing to families, the concept of children's meals wasn't yet widespread.

5
The Grand Seaside Hotel Today

By the turn of the millennium, although British seaside resorts were still attracting tourists, visits tended to be day trips and short hotel breaks throughout the year rather than one or two full week holidays in the summer. Reduction in visitor numbers at all seaside resorts led to further hotel closures as well as other attractions, and despite a recent resurgence in popularity, many resorts have yet to fully recover. As in previous decades, when resorts are in decline hotels are often converted into apartments or are demolished and their sites used for residential accommodation. Saltburn's Zetland Hotel was converted into flats in 1988, and the Ocean Hotel in Saltdean was sold by Butlins in 1999, and although it remained a hotel until 2005, it was subsequently converted into luxury apartments. Hotels elsewhere were demolished, including the Palm Court Hotel building in Torquay, which had been allowed to deteriorate over many years and was irreparably destroyed in a fire in 2010; its site was redeveloped with luxury apartments, and although it had not been a hotel for many years, the former Westward Ho! Hotel was finally demolished in 2000 and replaced with apartments.

The former Granville Hotel, Ramsgate, now apartments. Built as a terrace of eight houses in 1867 by Robert Sankey, John Barnet Hodgson and Edward Welby Pugin, who designed the building, the terrace was converted into a hotel in 1869. (Ron Ellis/ Shutterstock. com)

Above: A link with the past: stone from the demolished former Westward Ho! Hotel, Devon, was incorporated into the lower walls of the apartments built on the site, to the right of the photograph. (© Humphrey Bolton)

Below: The Abbey Sands complex, Torquay, during construction in 2014. It was built on the site of the Palace Court Hotel, which was destroyed by fire in 2010. Although its design arguably possesses a degree of Art Deco influence, the new building is very different in scale and design to its 1930s predecessor. (Torquay Palms)

Fortunately, many local authorities have adopted large-scale regeneration projects to stem decline and to reinvigorate seaside towns. In 2016 the British Hospitality Association proposed a Seven Point Coastal Action Plan that called on the Government to implement strategies to 'make our seaside towns destinations of choice for tourists and residents' and in 2017 it was announced that seaside towns will receive £40 million in Government investment to boost economic growth through implementing thirty coastal regeneration projects. £120 million has also been invested in 200 projects as part of the Coastal Communities Project since 2012, supporting 18,000 jobs and attracting £200 million in additional investment.

Holistic approaches to regeneration utilising all aspects of a resort towards attracting visitors are proving successful at places such as Weston-super-Mare, where it is recognised that the seafront's large hotels attract overnight visitors who then visit the town's museums, cinema and shops. Renovation of existing hotels and the construction of new ones also create jobs in the local area and provide a boost to the local economy, and so regeneration of seafronts where these showpiece grand hotels are located is often crucial to success. A major regeneration at Blackpool's New South Promenade included the demolition of several run-down and derelict hotels to make way for the 130-bedroomed Hamptons By Hilton hotel, which opened in 2018 at a cost of £8.5 million.

Culture and heritage values play a significant role in seaside regeneration, and instead of dwelling on 'faded glory', seaside towns like Margate, Hastings and Whitley Bay focus upon their heritage. Rejuvenation has helped to dispel stereotypical negative images of grim B&Bs and run-down promenades and arcades by introducing new galleries, quality restaurants and

An aerial view of Birnbeck Pier and Marine Lake, Weston-super-Mare. Regeneration projects at seaside towns incorporating the promotion of hotels for tourism can stimulate economic growth for other amenities, as at Weston-super-Mare. (Neil Mitchell/ Shutterstock.com)

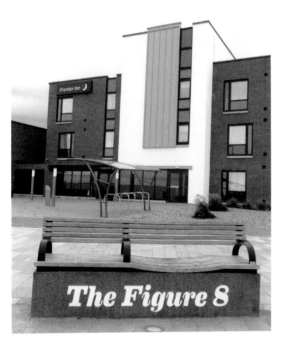

A Whitley Bay bench commemorating the iconic Figure-Eight Railway sits in front of the 2017 Premier Inn. Red brick was chosen as a main building material, as it is prominent in the local houses which form the area's general character. (© Geoff Holland)

destination hotels. In 2017 Historic England launched a collaborative initiative within several Heritage Action Zones across the country to identify, restore and revive neglected historic sites to attract businesses, investors, residents and tourists, thereby stimulating economic growth. Two of the zones are seaside towns, namely Ramsgate and Weston-super-Mare, which will continue to benefit from considerable investment.

Regeneration and investment in seaside towns attracts and motivates private sector investors willing to renovate and restore key areas in seaside town, usually the seafront, and often within the hotel industry. Both independent property developers and hotel chains are increasingly looking towards newly regenerated seaside areas that have benefitted from significant regeneration projects, including multi-million pound seafront redevelopments.

The revival of the seaside hotel industry has also been recognised by overseas investors, who play a significant role in the restoration and running of several historic grand hotels. In 2017 an overseas consortium acquired the Imperial Hotel in Blackpool and the Palace Hotel, Torquay, pledging considerable investment towards their redevelopment using local architects and consultants. The Riviera Hotel at Bowleaze Cove was purchased by an overseas investor in 2010, who undertook a multi-million pound wholesale refurbishment of bedrooms, restaurant, and ballroom and leisure facilities.

Did you know?

Some of Britain's seaside hotels have been used as locations for television and films over the years. The Headland Hotel, Cornwall, has been used as a set for many television shows and films, including *The Witches* (1987) starring Anjelica Huston. The Clarges Hotel on Marine Parade, Brighton, (now apartments) was once owned by actress Dora Bryan and was used for outdoor scenes during the filming of *Carry on at Your Convenience* (1971) and *Carry on Girls* (1973). Aberystwyth's former Queen's Hotel appeared in S4C's *Hinterland* as the police station, and in 2014 Scarborough's Grand Hotel featured in the BBC drama *Remember Me* starring Michael Palin and Mark Addy.

The Ocean Hotel, Saltdean, now apartments. The renovated and sympathetically restored 1930s building now has an additional storey, but this does not detract from its original character. (© Les Chatfield)

In an age in which competition for custom is fierce, upkeep of hotels, no matter what their age, is essential. Hotels today must compete not only with other local hotels, but other resorts and overseas destinations. Although many grand hotels are fully booked for the entire summer season, and remain popular for much of the year, accommodation has tended to be at the more affordable end of the spectrum with budget coach parties, mid-week specials including free nights as an incentive, and pre-season 'tinsel and turkey' and Twixmas breaks. Some hotels have gimmicks, such as the more modern Big Blue Hotel, Blackpool, next to Blackpool Pleasure Beach, painted a vivid blue. Other hotels at the more popular resorts keep running costs to a minimum, offering room-only accommodation, and tend to attract large groups of same-sex parties, popular with the hen and stag market. Other hotels attract a more mature and often retired clientele, offering full board mid-week deals, daily coach trips and evening entertainment, often bingo, and cabaret. This rather hotel-orientated stay echoes the early grand hotel experience, where stays at a grand hotel were hotel-centric, although the clientele and costs today are very different.

In contrast, there is a burgeoning niche market for smaller chic boutique or 'lifestyle' hotels, often with eclectic themes, which, although close to the sea, are rarely on the seafront and are usually located away from populist centres. It is often these smaller boutique hotels, such as Studland Bay's Pig on the Beach and the eco Scarlet hotel at Mawgan Porth, Cornwall, which command higher prices for exclusive, often child-free luxury, whereas the grand seaside hotels often have flexible deals and are often family-friendly. To address old-fashioned and cheap and cheerful images, and to attract a new clientele, several iconic grand seaside hotels have undergone transformations in recent years, with large-scale multi-million pound refurbishments and the introduction of new high-end facilities such as champagne bars and luxury leisure amenities. Spas, pools and 'award-winning' restaurants feature heavily in hotel brochures and advertisements, and one Brighton hotel has even advertised a yacht for corporate functions. Despite attracting a premium, rooms with a sea view remain high on the list of requirements for a stay at a grand hotel, and brochures invariably boast of 'stunning sea views'.

Business conference facilities and wedding packages feature heavily in marketing, usually with in-house catering as an essential. The latter proves especially lucrative, and almost without exception every grand hotel provides wedding packages worth thousands of pounds; large promotional posters or stands are often found within the hotel foyer with images of happy couples in their wedding finery. Afternoon teas are also heavily marketed, as are special occasion dinners such as Mothers' Day and Valentine's Day. Continuing in the seaside tradition of cartes des visites, many hotels continue to sell their own postcards as well as other hotel merchandise.

Despite the sometimes facelessness of corporate branding, many hotel groups recognise the heritage of their grand seaside hotels as a valued resource and incorporate past grandeur and history into their marketing. Original historic features have been retained, replaced and restored at many hotels, with varying degrees of success, historic photographs

Headland Hotel, Torquay, viewed from its gardens. Hotels with picturesque outdoor features are especially popular for summer weddings and add value to a hotel's desirability.

Right: Hotel merchandise can appear in various guises.
Below left: Original flooring at the Headland Hotel, Torquay. The conservation and preservation of original features are important in retaining a building's character.
Below right: The Royal Hotel, Weymouth, has many well-preserved features including fireplace detailing and fine exterior ironwork. (Jay Garrett)

of earlier incarnations adorn public areas, and brief potted hotel histories appear on many hotel websites. Links with the past are emphasised, especially regarding former famous guests or residents, such as Bleak House, Broadstairs, one of the town's many places associated with Charles Dickens, where guests can choose to stay in suites named after Dickens characters. Perceived or real links with royalty are commonplace, although sometimes facts mingle with fiction.

Awaiting the results of a facelift, 2017. Part of the extensive renovations to Brighton's Grand Hotel included re-rendering of the sea-facing façade, new windows and balconies and, interestingly, a new lighting system 'to enrich the architectural design of the building'.

The extensive refurbishment of The Grand, Brighton, between 2016 and 2018 played heavily upon its heritage; the Victoria Terrace Lounge and Bar in particular was designed around the hotel's original nineteenth-century architecture, albeit with a contemporary feel. The former Cumberland Hotel in Bournemouth, now a Premier Inn, has been successfully refurbished with its Art Deco origins in mind. One of the most successful restorations this century has been that of the Midland Hotel, Morecambe, completed in 2008 following a £7 million transformation project. The building had fallen into dereliction following years of storm damage and neglect, but property developers saw its potential for renovation and invested £7 million to restore it to its former 1930s glory, including conservation of integral art works which contribute to the building's character.

Given the tragic loss of so many grand historic hotels over the years, it is fortunate that many now have some protection as heritage assets, usually as listed or locally listed buildings, and are increasingly acknowledged within local authority legislation as being significant and integral to an area's built heritage and social history. Protection against detrimental development is increasingly important, especially when areas are being regenerated, and it is often recommended that restoration must account for a historic hotel's special architectural character and history, within both local and national contexts. Prominent seafront locations contribute to townscape value, which is one of the reasons The Grand Hotel, Tynemouth,

The Grand, Sandown, Isle of Wight. Although the significance of many historic seaside hotels is recognised, protection is not always guaranteed and this historically important hotel faced demolition for many years. (Phillip King)

was listed. For many years Lowestoft's Grand formed part of the Centre for Environment, Fisheries & Aquaculture Science Laboratory (CEFAS), but plans to demolish the modern buildings as CEFAS relocated excluded the former hotel due to its historical importance as a rare survival of a Victorian hotel in the town, and it is an important local landmark. As such, the local authority recommended its retention and that future conversion to tourist and/or residential accommodation should be sympathetic. When a former grand hotel is proposed for conversion, it is possible to preserve its original character, as was the case for Saltdean's Ocean Hotel, whose overall restoration was sympathetic, despite an extra storey being added.

As regeneration continues, new seaside hotels are being built all around the coast at key seafront locations, as at Exmouth and Whitley Bay, and they tend to be part of hotel chains and consortiums. Although some new builds receive criticism for their 'modern' design, this may be in part due to changes in familiar and much-loved seaside landscapes, but there is a visible trend towards more interesting and sympathetic design proposals, which take into account existing environs and prevalent local building materials.

The seaside holiday has changed, and the days of spending whole seasons in a grand hotel are now gone, as today's equivalent elite are more likely to holiday at exclusive overseas resorts, and most visits by those who do frequent the British seaside are unlikely to extend for longer than two weeks and are usually much shorter. This highlights the main difference between the older grand seaside hotels and those built more recently. The nineteenth and early twentieth-century grand hotels were exclusively for the aristocratic and wealthy and the wealthy middle classes, and the architecture and design of these hotels reflect this. As the twentieth century progressed, the wealthy holidayed elsewhere and the grand hotel became accessible to more people, but older establishments needed to modernise to compete with new seaside hotels, built for functionality. No longer the exclusive preserve of the wealthy, or restricted to hotel guests, these grand hotels are now widely accessible, whether for a traditional hotel holiday, a spa weekend away, an overnight business stay, or briefer visits for a luxurious dinner, an afternoon tea treat or a fancy cocktail. Lavish service, modern facilities, fine cuisine, tradition, heritage and architecture now form the grand hotel experience.

Jury's Inn Hotel, Brighton. Chain hotels today represent most new hotels built in prominent sea front locations, although many designs are more imaginative than in the later decades of the twentieth century. (Jay Garrett)

6
What Now?

The history of the grand seaside hotel is a fascinating one, both architecturally and socially, and each of the hundreds of hotels around the coast has its own unique story. There are no publications relating specifically to the history of the British seaside hotel, but they do feature within several more general works on hotel history and seaside architecture. Several hotel histories have been published over the years, a couple of which are included below.

Further Reading

Denby, Elaine (1998) *Grand Hotels: Reality and Illusion* (London: Reaktion Books). A thoroughly researched and detailed account of the history and architecture of grand hotel around the world.

Edwards, Jackie (2010) *A Bed by the Sea: A History of Bournemouth's Hotels* (s.l. Natula Publications). A detailed account of the history and development of Bournemouth's many, many hotels.

Freeman, Sarah (2015) *Beside the Sea: Britain's Lost Seaside Heritage* (Aurum Press Ltd). A great account of the golden age of Britain's seasides, focusing on nineteen resorts.

Gray, Fred (2009) *Designing the Seaside: Architecture, Society and Nature* (London: Reaktion Books). An excellently thorough history of seaside architecture.

Guise, Barry and Brook, Pam (2008) *The Midland Hotel: Morecambe's White Hope* (Palatine Books). A biographical history of the hotel including details of its rescue from demolition and subsequent restoration

Taylor, Derek and Bush, David (1974) *The Golden Age of British Hotels* (London: Northwood Publications). A solid account of the history of the British hotel 1837–1974 and the characters associated with them. Illustrated with photographs and useful drawings, all in black and white.

Perrett, Bryan (1991) *Sense of Style: Being a Brief History of the Grand Hotel, Scarborough* (s.l.). An informative potted history of the hotel.

Places to Visit

There is no substitute for visiting the real thing. Many historic grand hotels are available for overnight stays, weekend getaways or longer breaks, and deals are often available online via hotel comparison sites, as well as hotel websites. Although many hotels have been renovated and restored to their former glories, others retain a faded grandeur and the hotel guest experience will vary accordingly. Top tip: in older hotels, avoid rooms adjacent to the lift! Staying as a guest is not essential as most facilities are normally open to non-residents. Lounges, bars and restaurants are usually the areas of a hotel which are most sympathetically restored to their former glories, and drinks and meals can be enjoyed in opulent surroundings.

Get Involved

Historical Research/Hotel Histories:

There are several ways of finding out about the history of individual hotels. If they are listed, a brief description and some historical notes can be found online: https://historicengland. org.uk/listing/the-list/

Some hotels have had their histories published, including the Midland Hotel, Morecambe, and Royal Bath Hotel, Bournemouth, and most have potted histories on their websites, although they are sometimes brief and short on detail, with no historical sources cited and some inaccuracies.

Researching the history of a hotel can be very absorbing, and once it is acknowledged that not everything can be found online, visiting the local authority's archive and local studies or county record office is an excellent starting point: they will have historic photographs and key sources to help trace the history. Some hotel chains have their own archives, which can be used for research. Hiring a professional historical researcher or historian, such as the author, is another option: www.archangelheritage.co.uk

Hotel Architecture

There are several specialist interest groups and societies concerned with the preservation of historic buildings for all periods of architecture; further details including how to become a member can be found on their respective websites:

The Georgian Group https://georgiangroup.org.uk/

The Victorian Society http://www.victoriansociety.org.uk/

The Twentieth Century Society https://c20society.org.uk/

Seaside Heritage

For general seaside related heritage, the Seaside Heritage Network provides membership to professionals working with seaside collections and all those interested in seaside heritage and culture. Its aims include the promotion of the value of seaside heritage and culture and to share knowledge and expertise of seaside heritage. http://www.scarboroughmuseumstrust. com/seaside-heritage-network/